Joy

Also by H[...]

20 Days with David: Psalms f[...] Psalms 1-20

A Call to Christian Patriotism: A Weekly Devotional Essay Series

The Art of Aging

Christian Decision Making and the Will of God: A Practical Model

Curing the Heart: A Model for Biblical Counseling (with Bill Hines)

Grief: Learning to Live with Loss

Hope for New Beginnings (with Shirley Crowder)

James: The Other Side of the Coin

Life Lessons from Ancient Prophets

Paul the Counselor: Disciple-making as Modeled by the Apostle—edited by Bill Hines & Mark Shaw (Chapters 7 & 12)

Three to Get Ready: Premarital Counseling Manual

Totally Sufficient: The Bible and Christian Counseling (with Ed Hindson)

THIRTY SEVEN
Biblical Strategies
For Making Marriage
JOYFUL

Dr. Howard Eyrich

First published as *Route 37 to Marital Joy* by Growth Advantage Communication, 2022.

Published by Illumine Press, an imprint of First Half Leadership, 2023.

A CIP catalogue record for this book is available from the British Library.

ISBN: 978-1-7391698-6-2 (paperback)
ISBN: 978-1-7391698-7-9 (e-book)

This book is dedicated to the hundreds of couples who have allowed me to be their counselor. In His grace, God ministered to their lives through counseling.

He also ministered to me in two ways. First, He constantly reminded me to be judicious in implementing these biblical strategies/tools in my own marriage. Secondly, these couples were my teachers, ever pressuring me to sharpen my skills and to be attentive to God's Word, thereby enhancing God's gracious gifts for the benefit of His people.

About the Author

Dr. Eyrich's career has spanned more than sixty years. He has filled various roles including seminary professor and president, pastor, and church planter. He retired as the Director of Counseling Ministries at Briarwood Presbyterian Church, Birmingham, Alabama.

He has served as the Executive Director of the National Association of Nouthetic Counselors, and on the boards of the International Association of Biblical Counselors, Birmingham Theological Seminary, Trinity Seminary, the Biblical Counseling Coalition, and The Owen Center. He has also been a churchman serving on various Presbyterian Church in America denominational committees and Presbytery.

Dr. Eyrich and his wife Pamela have two grown children, eight grandchildren, four additional by marriage, and four great-grandchildren. Retirement for him is a time for ministry. He writes, teaches, preaches, and travels for the Kingdom. He also enjoys the hobbies of model railroading, hunting, and target shooting.

You can follow Howard on:
Facebook: facebook.com/howardeyrich
Blog: https://howardeyrich.com/category/marriage/

Contents

Introduction

US Highway 66, often known as Route 66 or the Mother Road, has a special place in the hearts of many Americans. Just the mention of Route 66 evokes images of simpler days, family businesses, and the iconic fuel stops and Coca Cola billboards.

In the same vein, here is a 'Route 37' mapped out for us in Scripture, to remind us that there are solid biblical strategies for Christian married couples to use, and which should have a special place in our hearts. Recalling and choosing to engage these God-given, incredibly simple, effective, and time-honored tools for relating in marriage will accomplish two very important goals for Christian couples. First, and foremost, God will be glorified by the way you treat your spouse. Second, these actions will facilitate marital joy for your spouse and yourself. We might add a third goal as well, mainly, modeling the practice before the next generation, providing them with positive impetus going into marriage, rather than saddling them with family of origin issues to plague their lives. This is also important as we see the pressure on marriages increase decade after decade.

The Status of Marriage in America

According to the new census data, the median duration of current marriages in the US has increased an exciting eight months in the last decade. It jumped from 19 years in 2010 to 19 years and 8 months in 2019. That is the good news of a recent analysis of the Census Bureau data. After a mix of somewhat hopeful data and discouraging data, here is the bottom line.

> "This sobering news about marriage puts a damper on our hope for the future of American families. With the rates of both divorce and marriage dropping in America, we expect to see the marriage divide deepen, as well as the poor and working-class Americans increasingly disconnected from the institution of marriage."

Other significant markers were these: sixty-four percent of college-educated professional people managed to keep their marriages reasonably stable. The problem with that statistic is that thirty-six percent did not. Working class folks fared less well at 24% maintaining their marriages.

The Status of Marriage in the Evangelical Church

The anecdotal observation is that those who take their faith seriously enough to attend church regularly and read the

Bible and related materials divorce significantly less than the general population. W. Bradford Wilcox, University of Virginia sociologist concludes that "active conservative Protestants", who regularly attend a church, divorce at a rate of 35% below the divorce rate of those who do not affiliate with a conservative church.

While these stats are worthy of note and we should rejoice, comparatively speaking, they paint a picture of a Christian population who fail to hear God and appropriate the resources He provides. The general statistic is alarming. Divorce occurred four times more often in 2018 than in 1900.

Here is the Good News

Those who regularly attend a church, read the Bible and pray, fare much better at maintaining a stable marriage. However, their lack of implementing the many resources that God provides in the Scriptures (and the means of grace resources it teaches) impairs their ability to grow in intimacy. Intimacy is a major source of comfort and confidence that yields joy, even in difficult times. The Family Institute study cited earlier found that there was a significant number of couples who indicated that their marriages were strengthened under the pressure of the recent pandemic, for example. I would venture a professionally educated guess that the reason this occurred is that these couples engaged in respectful, caring, problem-solving in everyday living.

How this Book Can Help You

As a *marriage enrichment tool*, any married couple—regardless of their age or the length of their marriage—can stimulate the growth and development of their relationship with God and each other.

As a *group study book*, it provides the opportunity for married couples to read, study, and implement biblical truths and practical applications during the week. Then they can come together with other couples to discuss what they learned and practiced in the past week and receive encouragement from other couples.

As a *counseling resource*, it is not a crisis-solving tool. Instead, this "coming-alongside tool" works in tandem with the crisis-solving tools. Working through this book, the counselor will trigger excellent homework for counselees.

Throughout the book, you will find questions to consider and answer. At the end of each Strategy/Tool, you will find blank lines to write notes, prayers, or important ideas you want to remember.

Here are the Key Resources God Provides (don't skip this bit!)

Scripture is based on the mission and grace of God. It is His story, His plan of redemption for the world. This includes His plan for marriage, which we find at the start with Adam and

Eve, and at the end with the final marriage: between Christ the Church, His bride. The grace of God was supremely displayed on the cross when Jesus died for His bride. He is a husband like no other! (Isaiah 54:5; Jeremiah 3:14).

If we forget the big picture or haven't grasped it, a book like this can end up becoming a list of rules, an assessment or grading tool, a how-to book separated from the golden thread of God's supernatural plan and provision. So to help us avoid the danger of what is called moralism (keeping various laws or rules in order to get right with or keep right with God) it's crucial that we are reminded that the bedrock beneath any commands in the Bible is the grace of God expressed supremely in the life, death, and resurrection of our Lord Jesus Christ, along with the power of the Holy Spirit to live out this new life in Christ, not "try and achieve new life". This includes the grace vital for living as a disciple of Jesus who is married.

Remember the lie to which the Galatians had fallen prey?

You foolish Galatians! Who has bewitched you? Before your very eyes Jesus Christ was clearly portrayed as crucified. I would like to learn just one thing from you: Did you receive the Spirit by the works of the law, or by believing what you heard? Are you so foolish? After beginning by means of the Spirit, are you now trying to finish by means of the flesh? (Galatians 3:1-3).

Below is a good example of taking a few commands in Scripture while forgetting God's gracious provision. If we read only part of the beginning of Peter's second letter, we can make it a list of rules and make the same mistake as the Galatians did and end up with graceless religion:

> ... make every effort to add to your faith goodness; and to goodness, knowledge; and to knowledge, self-control; and to self-control, perseverance; and to perseverance, godliness; and to godliness, mutual affection; and to mutual affection, love. For if you possess these qualities in increasing measure, they will keep you from being ineffective and unproductive in your knowledge of our Lord Jesus Christ." (2 Peter 1:5-8).

Let us remind ourselves of the words before (my emphasis in *italics*) and note what God has *done* for us in Christ Jesus.

> "Simon Peter, a servant and apostle of Jesus Christ,
>
> To those who through the righteousness of our God and Savior Jesus Christ *have received a faith as precious as ours*: Grace and peace be yours in abundance through the knowledge of God and of Jesus our Lord.
>
> *His divine power has given us* everything we need for a godly life through our knowledge of him who called us by his own glory and goodness. Through

these *he has given us his very great and precious promises*, so that through them you may participate in the divine nature, *having escaped* the corruption in the world caused by evil desires.

For this very reason, make every effort" ... etc (2 Peter 1:5-8).

Incredible isn't it? He is indeed the author *and* perfecter of our faith (Hebrews 12:2), the one who sustains individuals *and married couples* in their walk with the Lord. Let us lean on Him and the means of grace He has provided as part of His provision to enable us to live holy lives!

Having been set free from sin and given many precious promises in Scripture and God's enabling power, two key ways to access this grace is regular engagement in praying individually and as a couple, and regular engagement in community. If both spouses are committed to a vital spiritual reality and draw on this wonderful supply, they can virtually prevent divorce, and foster growing intimacy and joy. And when we realize which areas of our marriage we are failing in as we ponder again God's holy standard for marriage as we apply the tools in this book, let that realization drive us back to the cross on which the Prince of Glory died.

Here are thirty-seven strategies embedded in the Scriptures with which to unlock the joy and lock out the disappointment and disillusionment that lead to a hurtful, and eventually fractured, relationship. I will refer to these as strategies and/or as tools.

A dictionary definition of strategy is a careful plan or method for achieving a particular goal usually over a pro-longed period of time. As a plan, these thirty-seven serve as a manual for marital joy. As tools, they must be picked up individually and utilized appropriately in life situations. While these tools are addressed to the church to foster unity and joy in the church, they are directly applicable to marriage which is the smallest unit within the church (the church in miniature, if you please). These tools are made of the "one another" commands of our Lord.

How Do We Utilize This Book?

This is a great question! Regardless of how you are using this book (as a marriage enrichment diary, a group study book, or as a counseling resource), here is a suggested process, though you may find another way that works bet-ter for you. Begin by getting a copy of the book for each spouse (and one for the group host or counselor if there is one involved).

Below each "one another" you will find some space to jot down your thoughts. If you're reading this in e-book format, make a note somewhere of anything you've found helpful or provoking.

Step One: Husband and wife should read the entire book.

Step Two: Each of you should identify two ways in which your spouse has communicated love for you. Which tool have they consistently used well? The next time that happens be sure to make eye contact, share how they have affirmed their love for you, and thank them.

Step Three: Each should note the two "one anothers" that he or she recognizes as a deficiency *in themselves*.

Step Four: Each should write out a plan to address his or her own deficiency.

Step Five: Next, each should note the two "one anothers" in which they experience deficiency in treatment of themselves *by their spouse*.

Step Six: Each should be ready to suggest how they would appreciate their spouse addressing the deficiency.

Step Seven: Put aside the book and what you have written and pray over it for a week. Then review what you wrote and see if you still agree with yourself. If not, refine your responses.

Step Eight: Set a time to discuss the book and the four "one anothers" each of you have noted, with each spouse first focusing on his or her own deficiencies and plans for making a remedy.

Unless you are using this book as part of a group study, I would encourage you to agree on a place where you will regularly talk through these issues and not get distracted. This is discussed in the next section. After this, continue this process and work through each "one another" addressing all of them in terms of your relationship. It may take you a couple of months to complete the process.

Choose a Distraction-Free Location

Agree upon a location for a regular distraction-free conversation. Couples have reported that setting aside a particular place, maybe at home, a park bench, or perhaps a corner booth at McDonald's or a quiet cafe mid-afternoon has enhanced their ability to stay focused on the issue at hand and communicate respectfully as they work toward a solution together. Once you decide on the location, agree that you will also appeal to one another to meet at this spot when you find yourself agitated over an issue. Agree to make this your "sacred" location. Before conferring, always review the guidelines taken from Ephesians and James for godly communication. You will see these at the top of the section to follow headed, "How to Enjoy the Relationship You Create".

Couples who encounter communication challenges will find it helpful to have a regularly scheduled time to listen and talk with each other until the frequency diminishes.

Then they can move to periodic meetings and eventually meet only when one or the other requests to do so.

Our sacred place is: _____

_____

Our weekly meeting place and time is: _____

_____

The Purpose

These meetings provide a time and place for you as a couple to confer, not argue. Speak all the truth in love. Do not allow any concern to be carried over into the next day. Not all problems can be solved in one sitting. You may need to create an agenda and schedule the work over several sessions. Direct all your energies toward defeating the problem, not the other person. Your goal is to reach Biblical solutions, so always have Bibles available and use them to the best of your ability. (If you cannot cite Biblical references as a basis for a resolution, note these gaps; each should research to find references to share when you next meet.) Both spouses should keep notes that can be compared later if necessary. It helps to record the results of your work together.

> **Direct all your energies toward defeating the problem, not the other person.**

Since you, as a couple, seek Biblical solutions as you confer, the husband should take the responsibility to lead your time together. The wife should be active in the process since both spouses are created in God's image and should participate. Between the two, some simple but accurate notes will help any pastor or counselor sort out difficulties if you need their help—especially note proposed solutions and one or the other's objections. Open and close your time together with prayer.

A Useful Technique to Ensure Self-Control

Conferring is all about talking *together* and exchanging ideas, often with the intention of reaching a decision about something. If an individual argues, clams up, or does anything other than conferring, the other spouse must gently raise a hand or calmly indicate somehow that, "In my opinion we have stopped conferring." Whether the spouse who has raised their hand is right or wrong is irrelevant. The other person should then indicate if they are willing to calmly and actively continue to engage in the process.

How to Enjoy the Relationship you Create

The Basic Rules of Communication

From Ephesians 4:25-32 and James 1:19-2:6.

1. Stop lying and start truth-telling (Ephesians 4:25).

2. Keep current—the relationship, not necessarily the issue, is to be settled before ending the session (Ephesians 4:26).

3. Target the issue, not your spouse (Ephesians 4:29-30).

4. "Love-act", don't re-act (Ephesians 4:31-32).

5. Be quick to listen, slow to speak (James 1:19-20).

6. Control the tongue; control your life (James 2:5-6).

Strategy/Tool #1

Devotion

Be devoted to one another (Romans 12:10)

You engaged in this first "one another" we shall consider when you made a covenant with God in that first *marriage* vow. That commitment, made to God, was that you would be wholly devoted to your spouse. It is foundational for the marriage and all the other strategies.

Couples do well to attend a wedding at least annually, if possible, and allow themselves to engage attentively to the first two wedding vows. These two vows embody this "one another" in the marital relationship. The first vow is taken after the pastor asks something along the lines of, "Who gives this woman to be joined to this man?" Then each enter a covenant with God to take the other as spouse. This is followed by the second vow in which, before God, they vow to devote themselves to one another.

Devotion

Over the years, observing and performing weddings has regularly refreshed the wonder of God's design of marriage for me, and revived my responsibility for the covenant I made with Him, and with my wife Pam; hence, the practical recommendation for remembrance. As a sidebar, the Lord calls upon His people 8,670 times to "Remember", as a means of helping them stay on His prescribed trajectory for life. Remembering our vows is a good strategy!

_____

_____

_____

_____

_____

_____

_____

_____

_____

_____

_____

_____

Strategy/Tool #2

The Pledge

Be devoted to one another (Romans 12:10)

The second is a pledge based on the same Scripture as Strategy #1. This commitment is another dimension of that second marriage vow, in which we covenant with each other in the presence of God and before the congregation of witnesses. We pledge to keep ourselves wholly for our spouse. This is the very pinnacle of preferring one another in marriage.

Throughout the Old Testament, idolatry was the paramount issue for Israel. Idolatry was a matter of preferring someone (or something) before God and engaging in worship (intimacy) with that god. Paul teaches us that marriage is God's illustration of His relationship with His bride (Ephesians 5). Therefore, it is logical to draw the same application to the marital relationship between a man and a woman. Our preferring God over idols is a model for preferring our spouse over competitors.

_____

_____

_____

_____

_____

_____

_____

_____

_____

_____

_____

_____

_____

_____

Strategy/Tool #3

Have the Same Mind

Be of the same mind toward one another (Romans 12:16—NASB1995)

We sometimes colloquially express this as being on the same page with each other or having the same vision. This is not a matter of being carbon copies of one another. God is too good to make life that boring. Rather, it is about having a common spiritual framework for life. My friends (we will call them Jim and Sally) are a good example. They both enjoy going on cruises. Her artistic bent influences the choice of cruise destination and the cruise ship and the activities done on board, and his administrator/teacher bent (think: history) executes the planning. Their common spiritual framework sets the parameters for the activities and entertainment.

Having a common spiritual framework is the product of each spouse having a commitment to align his or her own mind with the mind of Christ. The Apostle Paul, writing to the conflicted Philippian Church, provides an exposition of being of the same mind toward one another. He begins his challenge with this appeal: *Make my joy complete by being of the same mind, maintaining the same love, intent on one purpose* (Philippians 2:1-12). Note that their getting on the same page would make his joy complete. So it is in marriage.

_____

_____

_____

_____

_____

_____

_____

_____

_____

_____

_____

_____

_____

Strategy/Tool #4

Accept One Another

Accept the one whose faith is weak, without quarreling over disputable matters (Romans 14:1)

The fourth addresses the common problem in marriage of operating on assumptions, which leads to making judgment calls about the motives of our spouse. We find it in Romans 14:1 and it underlines the importance of accepting one another by refraining from judgment. Whether reading a novel, watching a movie, or engaging in counseling with a couple, this is one of the commonly violated "one anothers". It always leads to hurt, disappointment, and wrong conclusions, which produce wrong actions.

Violating this strategy and failing to employ this tool is a hallmark of novelists and movie producers. A relationship is budding as the artist spins the story. Then, just when you think the relationship is going to come together, the heroine happens to glimpse the gentleman hugging a woman whom she knows was part of his past. She immediately assumes he is rejecting her in favor of his old flame. The artist raises the tension, but then relieves the tension several scenes later when his mother tells her, "Oh, sweetheart, what you saw was him congratulating her on her engagement. Her fiancé proposed to her during a video call last night from Syria as her Christmas gift." Her assumption, compounded by her judgment, triggered her purchasing a plane ticket home, an action she suddenly regrets.

In some marriages a spouse may bump into an old flame, which may cause the other spouse to think the worst of their spouse in this kind of situation. Unfortunately, it can become a learned pattern for some folks that haunts their marriage, especially after one spouse has broken trust.

The strategy here is simply a tool. When you see something that precipitates a question about a decision or behavior observed, pray for wisdom and grace, choose not to make a judgment call, and approach your spouse for clarification of his or her intent. It may sound like a wife saying: "Honey, I saw that you were talking with Jessica in a rather affectionate manner. I don't want to make a judgment call that there is something between the two of you, but if there is, please talk to me. I love you."

Strategy/Tool #5

Show Deference to One Another

Accept the one whose faith is weak, without quarreling over disputable matters. One person's faith allows them to eat anything, but another, whose faith is weak, eats only vegetables. The one who eats everything must not treat with contempt the one who does not, and the one who does not eat everything must not judge the one who does, for God has accepted them. Who are you to judge someone else's servant? To their own master, servants stand or fall. And they will stand, for the Lord is able to make them stand. One person considers one day more sacred than another; another considers every day alike. Each of them

should be fully convinced in their own mind (Romans 14:1-5)

Accept one another, just as Christ also accepted us, for the glory of God (Romans 15:7)

Accept one another by showing deference. This is the knockout punch for our self-centeredness and arrogance. This principle can have a variety of applications in marriage. A husband may find a pink living room intolerable. A wife may be very comfortable wearing feminine pants at Sunday morning worship while her husband is convinced that it is inappropriate. A wife may feel unsafe driving anything but an SUV. The list of possible conflicts is endless. The principle here is the responsibility of showing deference. While the context has reference to a weaker conscience, the principle is important in the broader application.

_____

_____

_____

_____

_____

_____

Strategy/Tool #6

Esteem One Another

Do nothing out of selfish ambition or vain conceit. Rather, in humility value others above yourselves (Philippians 2:3)

For by the grace given me I say to every one of you: Do not think of yourself more highly than you ought, but rather think of yourself with sober judgment, in accordance with the faith God has distributed to each of you (Romans 12:3)

The sixth is the opposite of esteeming oneself. The command can be summed up this way: Esteem one another in love. There is no competition allowed. To put it another way, think more highly of your spouse than yourself. See him or her as more important than you see yourself. A very practical rule is to never speak negatively about your spouse.

Rather, esteem the spouse in love by appropriately speaking to him or her about the matter of concern.

A circumstance in which this tool is handy is when one spouse is earning substantially more than the other. This situation may give the higher earner the opportunity to esteem herself above their partner. Their spouse, while not verbalizing it, may find himself despising the other for her superior earning power and her arrogance. This may be especially true for the husband (see the Appendix).

_____

_____

_____

_____

_____

_____

_____

_____

_____

_____

_____

Strategy/Tool #7

Build Up One Another

Let us therefore make every effort to do what leads to peace and to mutual edification (Romans 14:19)

... encourage one another and build each other up, just as in fact you are doing (1 Thessalonians 5:11)

These commands convey the imperative of seeking to enable your spouse to grow. Most couples come to marriage with a fantasy view of their spouse. The reality is that progressing in maturity both spiritually and humanly is the reality of being human. Tracing the three years of relationship between Christ and His disciples is to trace the growth and development of these men. When Christ chose them, they had not arrived; there was much growing to do. When a man or a woman chooses a spouse, that person has not arrived. As Christ built up these disciples, couples should build up one another. He loved them, taught them,

Joyful

corrected them, commanded them, sought them out when they sinned, and He forgave them.

Every couple should have, as a personal objective, the building up of their spouse. There are many opportunities. One place to begin is to not take their spouse for granted. This was something I had to learn. In my home of origin, both folks tended to take each other for granted. They seldom did for the other what they expected the other to do for them. Now, it was not meanness, it was neglect. Mom taught me to say, "Please" and, "Thank you" to others, but it was not part of our family conduct. My wife came from a family where these simple practices of building up the other by showing appreciation was the norm. My folks were not "bad people", they were working-class folks who were the product of the survival mode of the Great Depression.

> **Most couples come to marriage with a fantasy view of their spouse.**

Another simple example is a young husband caring for the children for an hour to give his wife the peace and quiet to read and pray or take time out to do some other activity. Since most mothers are the primary care givers for the couple's child(ren), it is when she is raising two, three, or four children; this is an opportunity to build her up spiritually, emotionally, and physically.

Strategy/Tool #8

Counsel One Another

I myself am convinced, my brothers and sisters, that you yourselves are full of goodness, filled with knowledge and competent to instruct one another (Romans 15:14)

It is possible because, as believers, we are on common ground. We have the Holy Spirit and the Word of God as our resource. As believers, we are equipped to be capable of counseling one another. For this to take place each must listen to the other, and each must seek to guide the other.

In addition to our spiritual capacities, we have different gifting and varying experiences. My wife's minor in college was public speaking. When I served as a young pastor her counsel was immensely helpful. Her training was a wonderful complement to the preaching classes I taught at a local Bible college.

_____

_____

_____

_____

_____

_____

_____

_____

_____

_____

_____

_____

_____

_____

_____

_____

Strategy/Tool #9

Serve One Another

You, my brothers and sisters, were called to be free. But do not use your freedom to indulge the flesh; rather, serve one another humbly in love (Galatians 5:13)

The next tool that was illustrated and taught by Jesus is servant leadership. It should not then be surprising that number 9 would be in God's toolbox for relationships. (This "one another" also sets the tone for prayer with sexuality—1 Corinthians 7:1-5.) Too often, the worldly tone frequently heard is the cry for "me" time that creeps into the fabric of the marriage. Obviously, there is nothing wrong with a man going hunting, fishing, or playing ball, just as there is nothing wrong with a wife going to a spin or other gym class or to a weekend trip with college classmates.

Each serves the other by supporting these activities as fulfilling and refreshing experiences. The key is effective communication regarding the when and how of these activities. We serve one another with mutual and clear plans coupled with adaptability.

There are a host of opportunities to serve one another in marriage. These opportunities are as simple as a man picking up his socks and tossing them in the hamper or wiping down the bathroom sink after completing his morning routine. Wives also have many mundane or casual opportunities.

Of course, serving one another calls for attentiveness to each other's life to identify when and how to serve. Capitalizing on these opportunities as a way of life enhances the ambiance of the relationship, generating a symphony of enjoyment as God intended.

Thinking of a symphony, one violin with one string out of tune is irritating and diminishes the enjoyment of the music. Similarly, certain habits, or lack of establishing certain habits, can irritate a marital relationship. Being self-aware of such habits or lack thereof and choosing to serve one's mate by sacrificing either the habit or the effort to learn a new habit contributes to marital harmony. You may be free to do otherwise, but in the process be selfish and fail to love.

The passage cited above means we do whatever is needed to help the mate. The whole Christian enterprise operates by servant leadership. A husband serving his wife does not violate his role as the head of the wife. Neither does the wife serving her husband encompass her entire role as a helpmate. For example, when our children were toddlers, on Friday or Saturday evenings (which one depended upon various factors), it was my custom to thoroughly clean the kitchen floor—whatever it took. Over the years, the demands of my ministry periodically kept me from attending to the lawn mowing schedule. My wife served me by mowing the lawn.

Having a mindset of serving will function as a radar to detect areas of service. A mindset focused on self will miss these opportunities and resent the times they obviously become a necessity. Earlier, Philippians 2:1-12 was cited. Revisit the passage; it pictures a mindset of serving.

_____

_____

_____

_____

_____

_____

_____

Strategy/Tool #10

Bear One Another's Burdens

Carry each other's burdens, and in this way you will fulfill the law of Christ (Galatians 6:2)

Different types of people need different types of help. This means that each spouse needs to be attentive to the other and learn their areas of weakness (burdens) that require help. It also suggests being attentive to undulating requirements, like a season of illness or temporary job demands, and taking the initiative to step in and bear a burden. For example, a wife who occasionally has a migraine will certainly need help at times bearing the burden of childcare or meal preparation.

A Respite and a Challenge

Let me challenge you to commit to studying, understanding, and then implementing this first set of strategies/tools. Use or adapt the illustration below. Make a duplicate and ask your spouse to evaluate you. Be bold enough to compare that evaluation with your own. Then, mark the three on which you scored lowest and write out a strategy to engage each one as a tool over the next three weeks. Continue this process over the next three weeks to establish a new habit. Pray for the Lord to help you humble yourself and exercise your commitment to honor Him and your spouse.

Directions: Circle the number that best represents an honest evaluation of how you are doing in living out each "one another" in your marital relationship.

1—Super bad | 2—Bad | 3—Getting by

4—Making progress | 5—Super great!

Be devoted to one another	1	2	3	4	5
Have the same mind	1	2	3	4	5
Accept one another	1	2	3	4	5
Show deference to one another	1	2	3	4	5
Esteem one another	1	2	3	4	5
Build up one another	1	2	3	4	5
Counsel one another	1	2	3	4	5
Serve one another	1	2	3	4	5
Bear one another's burdens	1	2	3	4	5

DIY Using the Manufacturer's Tools

Like every car, truck, computer, household appliance, or any other product utilized in this world, human beings come off the production line with fatal flaws. The manufacturers of these products issue manuals and tools necessary to gain the maximum enjoyment for the user and to ensure their own glory. The Lord of the universe, who ordained marriage before the Fall, provided a manual and tools to ensure maximum enjoyment for couples and to ensure His glory.

I trust that your experience with the personal evaluation of the first ten strategies/tools has convinced you that utilizing God's Manual is a wise choice. Consider now the next ten tools.

_____

_____

_____

_____

_____

_____

_____

Strategy/Tool #11

Be Gentle with One Another

Blessed are the gentle, for they shall inherit the earth (Matthew 5:5—NASB1995)

Be completely humble and gentle; be patient, bearing with one another in love (Ephesians 4:2)

Number eleven teaches us to practice the third Beatitude articulated by Jesus. In Ephesians, we are also instructed to be gentle with one another.

When picking up one of the model train engines on my model railroad, I do so gently. These engines have many delicate parts that can be easily damaged if not handled gently. Treating one another gently in marriage means to intentionally observe where my spouse is delicate and intentionally be gentle when addressing these areas. Another way of using this tool is for gentleness to set the tone of the relationship. It is much easier to process misunderstandings in an atmosphere of gentleness since there is no fear of a harsh response.

_____

_____

_____

_____

_____

_____

_____

_____

_____

_____

_____

_____

Strategy/Tool #12

Keep Applying the Glue of Kindness

Be kind and compassionate to one another ... so as to preserve unity (Ephesians 4:32)

Unity in marriage is essential. Even when couples are on the same page and have a common vision, there can be significant tension and disappointments regarding the manner of accomplishing the vision.

For example, both spouses may share the vision to have a family of four children. She may be ready to become pregnant immediately after marriage, while he desires to wait until he finishes his graduate degree. Utilizing this tool will help you to be verbally and emotionally kind in coming to a resolution.

There are many opportunities to be unkind. Colors in décor, hair styles, vacations, automobiles, to have or not to

have a dog (or two or three, as in my neighborhood), are just
a few common ones.

_____

_____

_____

_____

_____

_____

_____

_____

_____

_____

_____

_____

_____

_____

Strategy/Tool #13

Speak the Truth in Love

Speaking the truth in love, we will grow to become in every respect the mature body of him who is the head, that is, Christ (Ephesians 4:15)

Therefore each of you must put off falsehood and speak truthfully to your neighbor, for we are all members of one body (Ephesians 4:25)

Do not lie to each other, since you have taken off your old self with its practices (Colossians 3:9)

Number thirteen is a fine instrument necessary to assist couples in addressing the hard issues in their relationship. When you take that new car to the shop with only twelve thousand miles on it and your mechanic realizes that the problem is of your making because you have not been properly caring for the car, he will not be doing his job if he does not speak the truth to you.

Such is the case in marriage. God tells us to speak the truth in love. Speaking truth harshly or critically, or with a voice of disdain, will give your spouse occasion to be hurt and defensive.

My wife has often served to proofread my writing, and sometimes I have not invited her to do so. Those are times when I have crafted something to which I am attached. I am very satisfied (more likely, proud) of the way I penned that piece. Here is her approach: "Arkie (my nickname), you like the way you wrote this, but I need to point out that others are not going to be as proud of it as you are. Let me suggest ..."

_____

_____

_____

_____

_____

_____

_____

_____

Strategy/Tool #14

Mutually Submit

Submit to one another (Ephesians 5:21)

Some will object that this tool is inappropriate for the man in marriage. That is foolish. In the context, leadership is not the subject since the very next verse shifts to leadership by specifically citing the wife's responsibility to be under her husband's guidance. Verse twenty-one is about relationship function in fellowship (15-20). In fact, contextually, it seems best to understand this as mutuality in spiritual fellowship.

For example, my wife and daughter are readers. As does her mother, my daughter often shares the fruit of her reading of the Bible, spiritual books, and music that has blessed her. Both her husband and I submit to these women by learning from them. I frequently write out the product of my morning time in the Word, and she submits to listening to it and learns from it.

In everyday life, the fact of the matter is I don't know everything. It is not a compromise of my role as her head to submit to her wisdom, whether it regards the fabric of a new chair or not to attend a funeral when some flu bug is prevalent. (Let's remember that Moses was told to listen to his wife, Sarah, even though she was obedient to him—Genesis 21:12; 1 Peter 3:6. He was humble—Numbers 12:3).

Her godly wisdom is the product of the Spirit of God living in her, as it is in me. We complement one another by listening to and submitting to one another when it is the better part of wisdom to do so.

_____

_____

_____

_____

_____

_____

_____

_____

_____

Strategy/Tool #15–17

Keep Forgiving One Another

Therefore, as God's chosen people, holy and dearly loved, clothe yourselves with compassion, kindness, humility, gentleness and patience. Bear with each other and forgive one another if any of you has a grievance against someone. Forgive as the Lord forgave you (Colossians 3:12-13)

Numbers fifteen, sixteen, and seventeen are best seen as three aspects of one. These apply to both small and major matters in life. We are taught to: Remember the tool of compassion (Colossians 3:12), forbear with each other's human condition, and forgive sin (Colossians 3:13). Every spouse will sin against the other! Sometimes it will be an unkind word, sometimes squandering money on a selfish desire, and sometimes breaking the marriage covenant.

Compassion emerges from the humility of recognizing our own fallenness and the forgiveness granted us through Jesus' death on the cross, while forbearance is the exercise of the discipline to walk through the hurt and pain of restoration. Forgiveness is the choice to respond to repentance with the promise not to dwell on the offense, not to speak of the offense to the spouse or others, and not to use the offense as a weapon to manipulate their spouse on other occasions.

_____

_____

_____

_____

_____

_____

_____

_____

_____

_____

_____

Strategy/Tool #18

Speak and Sing Together in God's Presence

... speaking to one another in psalms and hymns and spiritual songs, singing and making melody with your hearts to the Lord (Ephesians 5:19)

Let the message of Christ dwell among you richly as you teach and admonish one another with all wisdom through psalms, hymns, and songs from the Spirit, singing to God with gratitude in your hearts (Colossians 3:16)

Engaging with other people as well as with one another in worship through music is number eighteen. Contextually this is about engaging together within the body of Christ for corporate worship. However, it is a wonderful way for marital spouses to worship together at home and to create an atmosphere of biblical admonishment in the home and family. This will go a long way toward influencing the young children born to them by both modeling and experiencing music that is uplifting, instructive, and worshipful.

_____

_____

_____

_____

_____

_____

_____

_____

_____

_____

_____

_____

_____

_____

_____

_____

_____

Strategy/Tool #19

Comfort Each Other with the Hope of Christ's Return

Then we who are alive and remain will be caught up together with them in the clouds to meet the Lord in the air, and so we shall always be with the Lord. Therefore comfort one another with these words (1 Thessalonians 4:17-18—NASB1995)

Number nineteen is always needed. However, in this unprecedented era of deconstruction of both the church and the society, a Christian couple will be drawn to one another and comfort one another as they ruminate on the hope of Christ's return, the reality that Paul has just discussed in 1 Thessalonians 4:13-17.

In his letter to Titus, Paul gives further insight into the value of this focus when he writes that the grace of God teaches us "to live sensibly, righteously and godly in the present age, looking for the blessed hope and the appearing of the glory of our great God and Savior, Christ Jesus" (Titus 2:12b-13). This passage identifies the "blessed hope" as the glorious appearing of Jesus Christ, our great God and Savior. In other words, contemplating this blessed hope that He could return at any moment gives Christian couples incentive to implement these tools. No one wants Jesus to appear in the middle of an ugly, dishonoring fight!

_____

_____

_____

_____

_____

_____

_____

_____

_____

_____

Strategy/Tool #20

Encourage One Another and Build One Another Up

Encourage one another and build each other up, just as in fact you are doing (1 Thessalonians 5:11)

John Gottman uses a scene from the book of Revelation to magnify his discovery of the four most destructive behaviors harming relationships in his *Cascade Model of Relational Dissolution*. They are Criticism, Defensiveness, Contempt, and Stonewalling. They follow in sequence and are all negative.

This is why the twentieth "one another" is so crucial. It is a tool that induces a positive sequence. Encouragement and building up fosters appreciation, which in turn, fosters admiration, which in turn, fosters intimacy. To encourage is a command. To encourage requires intentionality to both observe what can be affirmed as worthy and good and to overlook what is irritating. The more a spouse focuses intentionally on the positive and gracefully ignores the irritations, the more the spouse is encouraged to develop the positive. This enhances their attractiveness and the encourager's desire for intimacy with the encouraged spouse. My mother would have said it along these lines, "Son, the more you affirm her the more responsive she gets; the more responsive she gets, the more you want to affirm her."

_____

_____

_____

_____

_____

_____

_____

_____

_____

Implementation (Homework) 1

Here we again pause. Consider your marriage. Pick the two "one anothers" we have covered so far which you realize need development on *your* part.

Next, devise a practical, specific plan that will enable you to incorporate these two tools this week. Use the blank pages that follow and/or keep a separate journal of how your spouse responds to your obedience in utilizing these tools. This should be an ongoing process until the practice of each tool becomes a godly habit.

Or, if you tend to be a critic of your spouse, be observant of even the smallest things for which you can offer encouragement. Keep a journal of your spouse's responses. It may take some time to see or hear a recognition of your encouragement. Why? Because he or she has become accustomed to your negativity, resulting in a habitual response of ignoring what you say or hearing your voice and assuming whatever you said was criticism and not "building" him or her up.

_____

_____

_____

_____

_____

_____

_____

_____

_____

_____

_____

_____

_____

_____

_____

_____

_____

_____

_____

_____

_____

_____

_____

_____

In 1907, the hymn writer, Henry J. Van Dyke, penned the following from an old hymn that I love. It speaks of the Lord's wonderful ability to soften our hearts. This of course impacts our relationships, including our marriages.

> *Joyful, joyful, we adore Thee,*
> *God of glory, Lord of love;*
> *Hearts unfold like flow'rs before Thee,*
> *Op'ning to the sun above.*
> *Melt the clouds of sin and sadness;*
> *Drive the dark of doubt away;*
> *Giver of immortal gladness,*
> *Fill us with the light of day!*

They should certainly be our voice as we consider these tools provided by God to "melt the clouds of sin and sadness" in our marriages, as well as in our church relationships. Remember what I wrote in the introduction about the grace of God given us in Christ Jesus and the resources He supplies? The hymn reminds us that it's as we open ourselves up like a flower to the love of the Lord that He sustains us. Key means we are to include regular engagement in praying individually and as a couple, and regular engagement in community.

Strategy/Tool #21

Commit to Peace

*Live in peace with each other
(1 Thessalonians 5:13)*

This requires making a commitment not to fight. Growing up in a farming community mostly populated with various German and eastern European stock, I observed many couples who would have profited greatly from an intentional determination to live in peace with their spouse.

Couples frequently find it easier to fight than to live in peace. When queried, their responses often reveal pride, a need to be right, or a pattern they absorbed in their home life that led to their parents' unhappy marriage. About the age of fourteen, I stood on a hill overlooking six neighboring farms, where I had observed this conflicted atmosphere of troubled marriages. My frustration drove me to tell God, "If what these people have is marriage, you can keep it!"

Recently, my wife walked into the garage on a very wet and humid day as I helped her with a project on her car. She left the door open. As she approached the work bench, I said, none too kindly, "Close the door. Please." Immediately I saw the tension in her whole body, as she intentionally chose not to react to me and pour gas on the fire. In turn, I did likewise. I realized my mistake and she realized hers. We both chose to live in peace and let love cover one another's sin.

_____

_____

_____

_____

_____

_____

_____

_____

_____

_____

_____

_____

Strategy/Tool #22

Seek One Another's Good

Make sure that nobody pays back wrong for wrong, but always strive to do what is good for each other and for everyone else (1 Thessalonians 5:15)

This has two dimensions: One is seeking good for your spouse, the other is seeking good for your marriage. If each spouse has this two-dimensional goal, there will be some built-in protection from self-centeredness, the Wormwood[1] of marital relationships.

This seeking of good can be elaborate or simple. A man I knew who had the earnings of a corporate board member, chose to spend much of his income over several years escorting his wife to medical facilities worldwide to find a possible solution for her defective hearing. In another

---

1 Wormwood is the active demon in C. S. Lewis's *Screwtape Letters*. He uses it as a shorthand to cite Satan's strategies to tempt us.

case, a woman of limited means married a blind man and invested much of her life helping him to become a successful individual as well as a godly father. Both these individuals sought good for their spouse by being willing to sacrifice much of themselves.

_____

_____

_____

_____

_____

_____

_____

_____

_____

_____

_____

_____

_____

Strategy/Tool #23

Encourage One Another

Encourage one another daily, as long as it is called "Today," so that none of you may be hardened by sin's deceitfulness (Hebrews 3:13)

Everyone has a rough patch now and again. When a spouse encounters such a struggle, this tool should be utilized by the other, and be guided by many of the other tools such as gentleness, kindness, and love. This strategy is a special tool in a marriage that has incorporated the previous tools into the matrix of their relationship.

Sometimes a spouse may be captured by a blogger, or a preacher online or on the radio, who implants an unbiblical twist on a doctrine. Or, a spouse may not handle a personal offense from outside the relationship well and develop a hardness of heart. Times like this call for this tool to help the other forsake unbelief and so avoid developing hardness of heart. Notice, it is encourage—not demand, or command.

Encouragement may sound something like this to start the conversation: "Honey, I am not sure what is percolating deep in your soul, but I want you to know I am aware that you are hurting, and I am praying that the Lord will enable you to release it."

If the spouse reacts or clams up, it will be necessary to press forward something like this, "Okay, sweetheart, I took an indirect approach the other day and we are still stuck. I am aware that you have been listening to _____. I want you to make an appointment with the pastor to provide an opportunity one-on-one to walk you through _____'s teaching. Would please do that for me, for us?

_____

_____

_____

_____

_____

_____

_____

_____

Strategy/Tool #24

Spur One Another On

Let us consider how we may spur one another on toward love and good deeds (Hebrews 10:24)

This is about stimulating one another toward spiritual growth. As with the last tool, this one is most effective in a marriage context rich in the practice of many of the tools we've already looked at. Practice of the others creates a receptivity for this tool for stirring each other up. They create an atmosphere in which the one being encouraged is secure and feels fully accepted. This strategy can be employed in a variety of ways. For example, a wife/mother may assure her husband that she will happily handle getting their three children up, fed, and out the door for the next ten weeks so he can attend that early morning study each week to learn how to practice inductive Bible study.

Another example is a husband who travels for business two nights a week or occasionally for a week, and arranges his schedule to call his wife at a pre-arranged time. He will focus on hearing how her day went, hearing her concerns for the next day, and then praying with and for her. Depending on her response, he may also urge her to consider reading a passage of Scripture before bed or when she gets up, which is entirely appropriate as part of his overall concern for her. And if *he* has had a difficult day, she may well share a passage of Scripture for his meditation. Husband (and wife) may also share what they sense God has been saying to them that day in the Bible and in other ways to help encourage each other in their common faith. These kinds of actions involve considering, i.e. pondering ahead of time how we might encourage our spouse in his or her love for God and other people. Given the array of human interactions they each have, the different scenarios for mutual strengthening are endless.

_____

_____

_____

_____

_____

_____

_____

Strategy/Tool #25

Commit to a Local Church and Get Involved

... not giving up meeting together, as some are in the habit of doing, but encouraging one another—and all the more as you see the Day approaching (Hebrews 10:25)

This is a commitment to regular worship and support of a local church. Over my more than fifty years of counseling professing Christian couples, the failure of faithfulness to this commitment or the hollow fulfillment of this commitment has often been a core issue in the marriage. Far too many couples have tended to drift into a casualness toward their local church. The lake house, travel, a second job, late Saturday nights, sports, and a host of other priorities displace their regular engagement at church.

Others try and soothe their conscience by merely going to church and warming a seat during Sunday morning worship. Moreover, they are not engaged as Jesus prescribed in Matthew 22:37: "YOU SHALL LOVE THE LORD YOUR GOD WITH ALL YOUR HEART, AND WITH ALL YOUR SOUL, AND WITH ALL YOUR MIND."

Proverbs 13:15 describes the impact on their spiritual lives that sooner or later affects the marriage and the family. Consider my paraphrase of this verse, "Good sense and sound judgment produce a favorable lifestyle, but the conduct of the transgressor leads to calamity."

Newly married Christian couples, and those who become Christians along the way of life, will glorify God and enjoy the fruit of their faith in their marriage by the consistent and compassionate use of this tool from day one.

_____

_____

_____

_____

_____

_____

_____

_____

Strategy/Tool #26

Confess to One Another

Confess your sins to each other and pray for each other so that you may be healed (James 5:16)

This tool begins with the anguish often expressed as "Oh my, do I have to confess this to her or him?" The immediate context of this "one another" is physical healing. However, in the larger context of the Bible, the principle certainly applies to emotional and marital/relational wellbeing and healing.

Why should we consider confessing our sins one to another a tool for marital prosperity? The answer is simple. Confession is taking responsibility for an offense. Confession sets up the path of repentance. Confession and repentance combine as the foundation for seeking forgiveness, thereby providing opportunity for the spouse to grant forgiveness. In granting forgiveness, a pledge to dispense with the offense and never bring it up again is extended to the spouse. Hence, confession is the starting point for healing a ruptured relationship.

_____

_____

_____

_____

_____

_____

_____

_____

_____

_____

_____

_____

_____

Pray for One Another

*Confess your sins to each other and
pray for each other so that you may
be healed (James 5:16)*

In this same context James articulates "one another" number twenty-seven: Pray for one another. What is the best and first response for a spouse who causes hurt? The answer is to pray. Pray that the spouse will have a heart to forgive. Pray for a willingness to heal and reengage. These prayers prepare the offender's heart to confess and repent.

What should be the first response of an offended spouse? Guess what? Pray also! Pray for a heart of compassion and understanding. Pray that your spouse will understand that he or she offended and hurt you. Pray that he or she will listen to the Holy Spirit's conviction and confess, repent, and seek forgiveness. Also remember the truth expressed by Peter in 1 Peter 4:8, that "love covers a multitude of sins".

The writer of Proverbs describes the same tool a bit differently when he says, "A man's discretion makes him slow to anger, and it is his glory to overlook a transgression" (Proverbs 19:11). This is an internal tool that performs self-heart surgery. It is choosing to grant both mercy (giving what is not deserved) and grace (giving what is undeserved). In other words, it is choosing to forgive and not allow the offense (sin) to determine your response in the relationship.

_____

_____

_____

_____

_____

_____

_____

_____

_____

_____

_____

_____

Strategy/Tool #28

Patient Endurance

May the God who gives endurance and encouragement give you the same attitude of mind toward each other that Christ Jesus had, so that with one mind and one voice you may glorify the God and Father of our Lord Jesus Christ. Accept one another, then, just as Christ accepted you, in order to bring praise to God (Romans 15:5-7)

This tool should be one of the most used instruments. In fact, the appropriate use of many of the other "one anothers" will depend upon this tool's skillful, practical incorporation into the fabric of everyday life. Here Paul ends a long section about mutual acceptance between Jews and Gentiles, asking God to enable them to live in harmony, then telling them to accept one another. It is a reminder that we are to live by grace, not trying to fulfill commands or laws in our own strength (see Introduction).

Peter, who was writing to believers dispersed from Rome under the Emperor's persecution and living in very unhappy circumstances, encouraged this tool as a way of life (1 Peter). Marriage is a "kingdom on earth". As such, it will have the same stressors as any other kingdom. There are enemies without and enemies within. There are conflicts between friends. There are financial strains. There are pressures of the environment. Prevention of marital war and disintegration of the marital relationship requires a couple to be long-suffering and patient without complaint (1 Peter 4:9).

John Gottman writes about the results of not being patient and long-suffering as he draws upon a biblical allusion to the four horsemen of the book of Revelation[2]. He points out how couples begin with criticism (lack of patience), then cycle to defensiveness, followed by contempt and stonewalling. Rather than practicing patience and enduring some frustration while they learn how to process life together, their lack of patience and endurance gives way to talking about splitting up and eventually getting divorced.

Exercising self-discipline to practice patience and endure frustrations through the power of the indwelling Holy Spirit enables the Christian couple to mature in Christ

---

2 Gottman, John. The Seven Principles for Making Marriage Work. ISBN-10: | 9780553447712 | ISBN-13: | 978-0553447712

and to mature in unity. In the New King James version of the Word, the fourth element listed in the fruit of the Spirit is "longsuffering." The Greek word may be translated with several English words, but no matter how it's referenced[3], it is a vital aspect of the fruit of the Spirit for the body of Christ, including married believers. To be long-suffering or patient is to possess endurance. It is remaining in God's will, His character—love, peace, etc.—no matter what or how long we might have to endure something or wait for a promise. The result is a growing, enjoyable marriage.

_____

_____

_____

_____

_____

_____

_____

_____

3 The Merriam Webster dictionary offers "to be longsuffering, patiently enduring a lasting offense or hardship. Maintaining forbearance under provocation or strain without hasty or impetuous response."

Strategy/Tool #29

Be Humble Toward One Another

...all of you, clothe yourselves with humility toward one another (1 Peter 5:5)

The context here addresses three groups of people. The first is elders who are to humbly serve by being examples to those whom they shepherd or rule over. The second is younger men choosing to humble themselves by submitting to the leadership of elders. The third is this: "Clothe yourselves with humility toward one another." That applies to everyone in the church, which means it applies within marriage.

It takes humility for a well-educated woman to submit to her husband. It takes humility for a husband to accept the assistance or the role of a helper from his wife. She may have better financial sense or organizational management skills than he does. To humbly receive her teaching/

instruction or management as God's provision is a choice to apply this "one another".

My wife understood our children better than I did. She taught me how to relate to them. She has the patience of Job to keep up with the complexity of family finances. I humbly tell servers in a restaurant to give her the check because she is my CFO. By God's appointment I am the CEO, and she helps me get my job done; by God's grace, I humbly accept God's provision. In addition, she frees me to deploy my best gifts in God's service.

_____

_____

_____

_____

_____

_____

_____

_____

_____

Strategy/Tool #30

Be Affectionate Toward One Another

Greet one another with a kiss of love (1 Peter 5:14)

This governs affection and has several applications in marriage. First, in public, couples should demonstrate their godly commitment to one another by appropriate PDA (public displays of affection). Second, private affection should be demonstrated every day in a variety of expressions (like pet names, a gentle touch, soft verbal expressions, and kisses not linked to sexual pursuit). In the realm of sexuality, expectations and expressions should be respectful and executed in a manner that is well-pleasing to the spouse—think of the number of other "one anothers" like gentleness, kindness, care, etc.

Strategy/Tool #31

Walk in Fellowship with One Another

If we claim to have fellowship with him and yet walk in the darkness, we lie and do not live out the truth. But if we walk in the light, as he is in the light, we have fellowship with one another, and the blood of Jesus, his Son, purifies us from all sin (1 John 1:6-7)

With this tool we seek to engage in a godly walk with each other. Commentators differ on interpretations of this verse. Some writers take it to mean that fellowship or godly walk is with Jesus, while others understand that if we walk in the light as Jesus walks in the light, then we have fellowship, or a godly walk, with each other. I favor the latter meaning. Hence, each spouse must be responsible to walk in the truth (1:6) so that both are able to walk together in a godly fashion. Because we become one in marriage, a defection by either person impacts the other. Hence, to walk in godliness with each other, individually we must walk in godliness.

_____

_____

_____

_____

_____

_____

_____

_____

_____

_____

_____

_____

_____

_____

Strategy/Tool #32

Refuse to Become Resentful

Get rid of all bitterness, rage and anger, brawling and slander, along with every form of malice. Be kind and compassionate to one another, forgiving each other, just as in Christ God forgave you (Ephesians 4:31-32)

Oh, how important number thirty-two is! Refuse to become resentful toward one another as Cain was of Abel (Genesis 4:1-8; John 3:11-12). Ephesians 4:31-32 highlights the importance of this tool in offsetting a naturally destructive and sinful pattern which affects a harmonious relationship.

The Greek language in v31 suggests a progressively escalating intensity of destructive behavior that looks like this: bitterness > rage > anger > brawling > slander > malice. Resentment is the starting point of *bitterness*. Unchecked bitterness leads to an internal agitation (*anger*). Left unchecked this *anger* flows outwardly as expressed *anger*, which bursts forth in loud yelling (brawling); this progresses into *slander* (blaspheme in the Greek) and finalizes as *malice*, that is, intent to hurt.

Verse 32 explains how we implement this tool. The manner of use has already been discussed in previous "one anothers".

_____

_____

_____

_____

_____

_____

_____

_____

_____

_____

_____

_____

Strategy/Tool #33

Lay Down Your Lives for One Another

This is how we know what love is: Jesus Christ laid down his life for us. And we ought to lay down our lives for our brothers and sisters. If anyone has material possessions and sees a brother or sister in need but has no pity on them, how can the love of God be in that person? (1 John 3:16-17)

A different phrase for this strategy is: Give of yourself for the sake of your spouse. The Apostle John articulates this, though he does not use the exact "one another" phrase, but by implication the meaning is present. Ponder the verses above.

Give sacrificially to meet the needs of your spouse. This principle in action will prevent one's indulgence at the expense of limiting the legitimate needs of your spouse, i.e. just doing the minimum needed. Love means pouring out, not doing the least possible. This laying down of one's life has of course particular application to the husband (Ephesians 5:25—the giving up of self for your wife).

The value of this tool is two-fold. First, it honors God by obedience. Second, it serves their spouse by removing an occasion for resentment and the escalation mentioned in tool 32.

_____

_____

_____

_____

_____

_____

_____

_____

_____

_____

_____

Strategy/Tool #34

Fight Fear with Love

There is no fear in love. But perfect love drives out fear, because fear has to do with punishment. The one who fears is not made perfect in love (1 John 4:18)

In 1 John 4:15-21 in which this sentence sits, the "one another" phrase does not occur but is implied. This tool is only available to the one who confesses that Jesus is the Son of God and therefore lives accordingly (v15). The tool may be summarized from this passage: Join together as a couple and fight fear by growing in love. There is way too much richness in the theology of these verses to be explored in this brief treatise. Suffice it to say, that growing in love for God, who first loved us, proportionately diminishes fear. In parallel manner, growing in love for one another in marriage diminishes the fear of facing the challenges of life together.

We grow in our love for God through growing in our knowledge of Him by practicing intimacy with Him through prayer, the Word, and the sacraments. In a similar manner, we grow in love by getting to know each other by cultivating intimacy through engagement in every dimension of life together.

_____

_____

_____

_____

_____

_____

_____

_____

_____

_____

_____

_____

Strategy/Tool #35

Appreciate your Differences

... so that there should be no division in the body, but that its parts should have equal concern for each other (1 Corinthians 12:25)

The focus of the context is the local church and schism. Church schism is more often about demanding personal preference than about infidelity to doctrine. It leads to pride and devaluing the other. This same culprit divides marital spouses.

The principle is applicable to the smallest unit of the church: marriage. However, the simplicity of Scripture is the answer in both cases. Recognize that differing gifts are from God. Recognize that preferences are cultural in origin. Accept these realities and celebrate them by being concerned for one another. This concern will curb your demands and will not only help you listen but cultivate an appreciation for the differences between you. How is your spouse gifted?

_____

_____

_____

_____

_____

_____

_____

_____

_____

_____

_____

_____

_____

_____

_____

_____

_____

_____

Strategy/Tool #36

Show Hospitality Toward One Another

Offer hospitality to one another without grumbling (1 Peter 4:9)

On the couple relationship level, welcome your spouse into every aspect of your life—no secret rooms. On the couple community level, together engage your community in your home and lives. It enriches your relationship with fellowship, fun, and growth through challenges.

My wife and I have countless illustrations of this dynamic. As my wife presented a women's seminar, she shared our practiced hospitality. Afterward, a woman asked, "Do you ever entertain strangers?" Pam answered, "There have been those who were strangers when entering, but left as friends."

My daughter came to Christ as a five-year old after we had a summer intern (stranger when he came, friend when he left) live with us. The conversations around the lunch and dinner table of his canvassing the neighborhoods and witnessing, prepared her heart to realize that, "her heart was black and needed Jesus to wash it white with His blood". Three years later she led her five-year-old brother to faith in Christ.

_____

_____

_____

_____

_____

_____

_____

_____

_____

_____

_____

_____

Strategy/Tool #37

Demonstrate Mutual Love and Respect for One Another

However, each one of you also must love his wife as he loves himself, and the wife must respect her husband (Hebrews 5:33)

Our final principle is to love and respect one another. Love and respect are interrelated. Love one another selflessly and treat one another with respect.

If left unchecked, we can easily fall into a sinful pattern of showing disrespect to our spouse. We must be cognizant of our actions and intentional as we strive to treat our spouse with respect.

Show respect as you acknowledge and value your spouse's opinions, feelings, and unique contributions to your relationship. First Peter 3:7 reminds us that husbands and wives have equal standing before God are co-heirs of the "gracious gift of life."

When you treat one another with respect, you can build a strong and enduring relationship that reflects God's love and grace.

_____

_____

_____

_____

_____

_____

_____

_____

_____

_____

_____

_____

Implementation (Homework) 2

Now that you have reviewed all 37 strategies/tools consider once again how you might implement these in your marriage. Choose the two "one anothers" you realize are most frequently missing in the daily context of your relationship. Next, devise a practical, specific plan that will enable you to incorporate these two tools this week. Use the blank pages that follow and/or keep a journal of how your spouse responds to your obedience in utilizing these tools. This should be an ongoing process until the practice of each tool becomes a godly habit.

Or, if you tend to be a critic of your spouse, be observant of even the smallest things for which you can offer encouragement. Keep a journal of your spouse's responses. It may take some time to see or hear a recognition of your encouragement. Why? Because he or she has become accustomed to your negativity, resulting in a habitual response of ignoring what you say or hearing your voice and assuming whatever you said was criticism and not "building" him or her up.

_____

_____

_____

_____

_____

_____

_____

_____

_____

_____

_____

_____

_____

_____

_____

_____

_____

_____

_____

_____

Appendix

Carly Fiorina is one of the most accomplished women in America. She holds degrees from America's most prestigious schools. After graduating from Stanford University in 1976 with a bachelor's degree in medieval history and philosophy, she attended law school at the University of California, Los Angeles, but dropped out after only one semester. She later studied at the University of Maryland, College Park (M.B.A., 1980), and at the Massachusetts Institute of Technology's Sloan School of Management (M.S., 1989). She rose through business ranks to become the CEO of Hewlett Packard and entered the 2016 presidential election cycle.

Her husband, Frank, grew up blue collar and started his career with AT&T as a truck driver/technician. He worked his way up into management where he and Carly worked together.

My brief research indicated that Frank is a believer as is Carly. According to *The New York Times*, she told Iowa's Faith and Family Forum, "It was my husband Frank's and my personal relationship with Jesus Christ that saved us from a desperate sadness," commenting on the loss of their daughter (her stepdaughter, referred as our daughter) to a drug overdose.

They make an ideal example of a couple who esteem the other more than themselves. Here are some excerpts from a CNN interview when she bid for the Republican nomination.

While some men might be intimidated, or even put off by being Mister Carly Fiorina, he says he "was always proud to be."

Frank even quit his own impressive corporate job at age 48 when she became CEO of Hewlett Packard, in order to be there for her.

"It was quite controversial, believe me. I knew it was the right thing to do," Frank told us in an interview at his wife's campaign headquarters.

He said his friends were split "50-50" about whether it was the right thing to do. Some were jealous, others thought he was nuts. But he was surprised by the person most upset about his decision to give it all up for his wife— Carly's father.

"[He was a] very accomplished man—law professor and federal judge—he could not understand how I could give up my career to support my wife," recalls Frank.

"Several years later he came around and he thanked me over and over for doing just that. Because he knew it was the right thing for Carly and the support she needed," he added.

Scripture Index

Scripture Index

Joyful